P9-DGE-453

Look What Came From Mexico

by

Miles Harvey

Franklin Watts
A Division of Grolier Publishing
New York London Hong Kong Sydney
Danbury, Connecticut

Series Concept: Shari Joffe
Design: Steve Marton

Library of Congress Cataloging-in-Publication Data

Harvey, Miles.
Look What Came From Mexico / by Miles Harvey.
p. cm. – (Look what came from)
Includes bibliographical references and index.
Summary: Describes some familiar foods, arts and crafts, music, sports, holidays, and more that originated in Mexico.
ISBN 0-531-11496-1 (lib. bdg.) 0-531-15939-6 (pbk.)
1. Mexico–Civilization–Juvenile literature. 2. Civilization–Mexican influences–Juvenile literature. [1. Mexico–Civilization. 2. Civilization–Mexican influences.] I. Title. II. Series.
F1210.H34 1998
972–dc21 97-30825
CIP
AC

Photo credits ©: Animals, Animals: 20 left (Michael Fogden), 20 right (Robert Pearcy), 21 right (George H. Huey); Ben Klaffke: stamp on back cover, 3 bottom, 18 middle, 18 right; Charise Mericle: 5; Dave G. Houser: 9 left (Jan Butchofsky), 16 right (Steve Cohen); Ed O'Shaughnessy/O Productions: 4 right, 6 right; E. T. Archive: 7 right, 11 bottom left; Envision: front cover top right, front cover bottom right, 8 left, 22 middle, 22 right (Steven Needham), 1, 6 left (Melabee Miller), 7 middle, 32 left (George Mattei), 9 right (Tim Gibson); The Image Works: 8 right (Esbin-Anderson), 11 right, 14 right, 15 (B. Daemmrich), 17 (Macduff Everton), 25 top (Mark Godfrey); International Stock: 21 left (Steve Myers), 3 top, 14 left (Cliff Hollenbeck), 18 left, 25 bottom (George Ancona), 22 left (Ron Sanford); Gamma-Liaison International: 24 left (Ellen Dooley); Omni-Photo Communication: 24 right (Esbin-Anderson); Photographers/ Aspen: 19 right (David Hiser); Photo Researchers, Inc.: 10 left (Dana Hyde), 12 left (R. C. Hermes), 23 (David M. Grossman); Rengin Altay: 32 right; Southern Stock Photo Agency: 27 (Index Stock Photography, Inc.); SuperStock: 13 bottom (Underwood Photo Archives, San Francisco, CA); Tony Stone Worldwide: front cover background, 12 right, 13 top (Robert Frerck), 11 top left (Oliver Benn), 16 left (David Hiser); Viesti Associates, Inc.: border on 4, 6-32 (Michael Lewis), 4 left, 19 left (Richard Pasley), 4 middle (Joe Viesti)

Printed in the United States of America.
1 2 3 4 5 6 7 8 9 10 R 07 06 05 04 03 02 01 00 99 98

Contents

Marvelous Mexico

Mexico is a huge and beautiful country just south of the United States. It has an amazing history. Mexico was home to several great civilizations. One of these was called the Mayan empire. It began about 2,300 years ago and came to an end about 1,100 years ago. Another was called the Aztec empire. It began about 600 years ago and came to an end almost 500 years ago. These Mexican civilizations had incredible cities and fantastic art.

Almost 500 years ago, Spanish explorers came to Mexico and claimed it as part of Spain. Mexico was ruled by the Spanish until 1821, when it became an independent country.

Today, Mexico is a mix of Spanish and Native American cultures. Nearly 100 million people live there. But millions of other people whose families come from Mexico now live in the United States and Canada. Let's find out about all the amazing things that come from Mexico!

The flag of Mexico

Mexican coins and paper money

UNITED STATES
RIO GRANDE
MEXICO
chocolate
piñata
GULF OF MEXICO
PACIFIC OCEAN
Chili peppers
GUADALAJARA
MEXICO CITY
rebozo
Sombrero
GUATEMALA
chihuahua
N
W
E
S

Food

Squash

The Mexicans were among the world's first farmers. About 10,000 years ago, people in Mexico began growing **squash.** Today, people all over the world love to eat this delicious and healthy vegetable.

Many other yummy foods also come from Mexico. Have you ever tried **chili peppers?**

Woman selling chili peppers

In Mexico, they're called *chiles.* They're delicious—but be careful. They can really make your mouth sting! Mexicans have been eating chili peppers for about 9,500 years. Today, some of the spiciest chili peppers in the world come from Mexico. Mexicans use them in many different kinds of meals.

Habaneros, the hottest of all chili peppers

Aztecs harvesting corn

Mexicans came up with the idea of growing **corn** for food about 4,500 years ago. Before that, corn plants grew in the wild in Mexico for at least 80,000 years!

Almost everybody loves **chocolate.** People in Mexico first began making chocolate about 1,900 years ago. During the Mayan empire, chocolate was so popular that people used it as money!

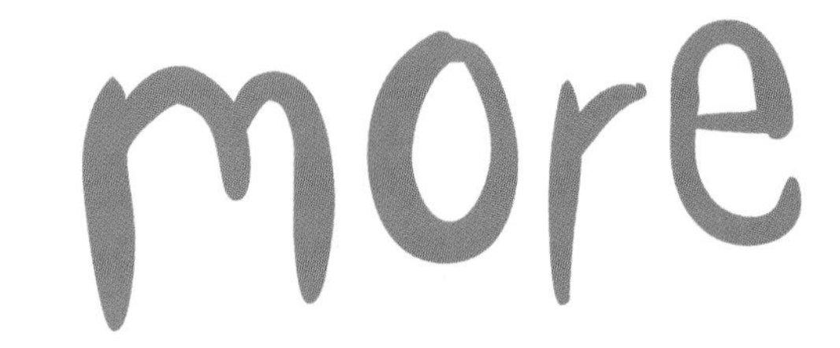

Tamales come from Mexico as well. These treats are made from a special corn dough and are often served in a corn husk. Another popular Mexican food is called the **tortilla.** It is a flat, round-shaped bread. Tortillas are often made from corn that has been ground up into a flour.

Chocolate

Tamales

food

Woman making tortillas

Tacos

Tacos are made from tortillas that are folded in half and filled with meat and vegetables. Today, many people in North America enjoy eating this tasty Mexican meal.

Fashion

Serape

People in Mexico have been weaving beautiful fabrics for thousands of years. One traditional product made from these fabrics is the **serape.** A serape can be worn as a coat or used as a blanket.

Many other wonderful kinds of clothing also come from Mexico. The **sombrero** is a very famous kind of Mexican hat. The top of this hat can be very tall, and the brim is very wide. Sometimes people have to take their sombreros off so that they can fit through a doorway!

Sombreros

Morral

Some Mexicans make colorful, rectangular bags called **morrales.** These bags can be worn as purses or used to carry groceries or other items.

A shawl is a type of clothing that you wear over your shoulders. Women in Mexico sometimes wear a traditional shawl called a **rebozo.** It can be worn many different ways. It can even be used as a kind of hat!

People wearing rebozos

Inventions

The Mayan Indians invented **chewing gum** more than 1,000 years ago. They made gum out of a liquid that comes from a tree called the sapodilla.

Mexicans also invented the first **rubber balls.** In ancient Mexican civilizations, people used these balls to play a game called *tlachtli.* In some ways, this game was like basketball.

Sapodilla tree

Ruins of an ancient Mexican ball court

Stone "hoop" used in the ancient game of tlachtli

Ancient Mexicans playing tlachtli

Music

Lots of Americans love the music of Mexico. In fact, many big cities have radio stations that play Mexican music all day long. One of the most famous kinds of music from Mexico is called **mariachi.** People who play in mariachi bands often wear special uniforms called *charro* suits. Mariachi bands play at dances, festivals, weddings, and other events.

A special instrument used in mariachi music is the **guitarron.** It looks a lot like a guitar, but it has a bigger body and smaller neck. The guitarron makes a deep, clear sound. Another mariachi instrument is called the **vihuela.** It looks like a tiny guitar. But a guitar has six strings, while the vihuela has only five. The vihuela makes a beautiful, high-pitched sound.

Guitarron

Mariachi band

The instrument on the left is a vihuela.

Sometimes masks are used during religious festivals in Mexico.

Arts and Crafts

Mexican animal mask

Mexicans did not invent **masks,** but they have been making them for more than 3,000 years. Today, many people in North America collect masks made by artists in Mexico. Some of these masks look like people. Others look like animals, such as pigs, bulls, tigers, and alligators. Some masks even look like devils or monsters!

Bowls made out of squash plants

Lots of people also collect other beautiful types of arts and crafts made in Mexico. For example, Mexican artists make pretty **squash-plant** bowls. They take all the pulp out of the middle of the plant, dry the plant, and then paint the whole thing.

The Tarahumara people in northern Mexico are famous for their beautiful **yucca baskets.** Yucca is a kind of plant that grows in the desert.

Yucca baskets

Toys

Have you ever played with a **piñata?** It is a very unusual kind of toy. On the outside, it looks like a beautiful bird or other colorful creature. On the inside, it is filled with candy. On Christmas Eve, Mexican children play a fun game that involves a piñata. They hit the piñata with sticks until it breaks apart. Then the candy comes falling out and all the kids get to eat it!

Piñata

Another interesting Mexican toy is the clay **chia pet.** You wet the chia pet with water and rub seeds onto it. Within a few weeks, it grows "fur" made of hundreds of tiny little plants!

Chia pet before and after it grows its "fur"

One of the most interesting parts of Mexico is a region called Oaxaca. Artists in Oaxaca are famous for creating **handmade dolls.** These dolls are often made of wood and are painted in beautiful and unusual colors.

Oaxacan wooden dolls

Many of them look like bulls, lions, lizards, giraffes, or other animals.

Animals

One of the most amazing animals found in Mexico is the **resplendent quetzal.** During the Mayan and Aztec empires, people worshiped this beautiful bird as a god. Today, however, there are not that many resplendent quetzals still alive. That's because people keep cutting down the forests where these incredible animals live.

Many other interesting animals also come from Mexico, including the smallest kind of dog in the world. It is called the **Chihuahua.**

Resplendent quetzal

Chihuahua puppies

Monarch butterfly

Even when it is grown up, a Chihuahua weighs only about 5 pounds (2.3 kg)!

Each spring, millions of eastern **monarch butterflies** fly from Mexico to the United States. These incredible insects can fly as far as 4,000 miles (6,436 km), and travel up to 80 miles (129 km) a day!

Another cool Mexican animal is the **Bolson tortoise.** It is the largest land-living reptile in North America, and can be found only in the Mexican desert. To protect itself from its enemies and the harsh temperature of the desert, this amazing animal sometimes digs holes in the ground that are 26 feet (8 m) long and almost 7 feet (2 m) deep!

Bolson tortoise

Words

Several words that we use all the time come from Mexico. One of them is **"coyote,"** the name for a North American animal related to the wolf. We get this word from the Aztec Indians. Another word that we get from the Aztecs is **"tomato."** People in Mexico love to put tomatoes in all different kinds of meals.

Tomatos

"Cocoa" is a delicious hot drink that tastes like chocolate! This word also comes to us from the Aztecs.

Coyote

Cocoa

A **"cafeteria"** is a restaurant where people serve themselves and take food to tables to eat. Does your school have a cafeteria? This word was created by the Spanish-speaking people of Mexico.

Cafeteria

Festivals and Holidays

Cinco de Mayo parade

Mexican Independence Day celebration

Mexicans celebrate some of the same holidays we do. But they also have some incredible celebrations all their own. One of them is called **Cinco de Mayo,** which means "Fifth of May" in Spanish. On that day in 1862, Mexican soldiers defeated French troops in an important battle. Today, this victory is celebrated with parades, dances, parties, and fireworks. Cinco de Mayo is also celebrated by Mexican-Americans living in the United States and Canada.

On September 15 and 16, Mexicans celebrate **Mexican Independence Day.** This holiday commemorates Mexico's declaration of independence from Spain. Spain had ruled Mexico from 1521 until 1821.

On November 2, Mexicans celebrate an amazing holiday. It is called the **Day of the Dead.** The purpose of this holiday is for people to honor their friends and relatives who have died. Many people observe this holiday by making masks, toys, and candy that look like skeletons.

On the Day of the Dead, people bring food, presents, and candles to the graves of loved ones who have died.

A Recipe from Mexico

When Spanish explorers arrived in Mexico more than 400 years ago, they found the Aztec Indians eating a delicious green fruit called the **avocado.** Today, the avocado is used in many Mexican dishes—especially a yummy treat called guacamole (pronounced gwah-cah-MOH-lay). You can make guacamole yourself, with the help of an adult.

Guacamole

To start, you'll need the following ingredients:

1 lemon or lime
2 medium-sized ripe avocados (Before you buy the avocados, you should give them a little squeeze. They should feel soft. If they feel hard, they're not ripe enough.)
1 or 2 medium cloves of garlic
1/2 teaspoon of salt
1 bag of your favorite tortilla chips

If you like food a little spicy, you might also want to use the following ingredients:

1/2 teaspoon of cumin
1/2 teaspoon of chili powder

You'll also need the following equipment:

1 cutting knife (to be used only with adult supervision)
1 cutting board
1 medium-sized shallow bowl
1 large fork
1 large spoon

You can make the guacamole by yourself, with an adult watching.

1. Wash your hands.
2. Peel the skin off the garlic.
3. Making sure to keep your fingers out of the way of the blade, cut the garlic into very tiny pieces. This kind of cutting is called mincing.
4. Cut the lemon or lime in half and squeeze 2 tablespoons of juice into the bowl.
5. Cut the avocados in half, remove the pits, and spoon the soft green part into the bowl.
6. Using the fork, mash the avocado and juice together until the mixture is soft.
7. Stir in the garlic and salt. If you want the guacamole to be a little spicy, stir in the cumin and chili powder.
8. Dip a tortilla chip into the guacamole and taste. You're ready to eat a delicious snack!

How do you say...?

People in Mexico speak Spanish. Try saying some words in Spanish for yourself!

English	Spanish	How to pronounce it
hello	buenos días	BWAY-nos DEE-ahs
goodbye	adiós	ahd-dee-OHS
please	por favor	POR fah-VOR
thank you	gracias	GRAH-see-us
ball	pelota	pay-LOW-ta
butterfly	mariposa	mar-ee-PO-sa
chewing gum	chicle	CHEE-clay
corn	maíz	ma-EES
chocolate	chocolate	choc-o-LOT-ay
dog	perro	PE-row
music	música	MOOZ-ee-ca

To find out more

Here are some other resources to help you learn more about Mexico:

Books

Defrates, Joanna. **What Do We Know About the Aztecs?** Peter Bedrick Books, 1992.

Irizarry, Carmen. **Passport to Mexico.** Franklin Watts, 1994.

James, Ian. **Inside Mexico.** Orchard Books, 1989.

Titor, Pilar. **Mayan Civilization.** Children's Press, 1993.

Wood, Tim. **The Aztecs.** Viking, 1992.

Organizations and Online Sites

Mexican Cultural Institute
2829 16th Street, NW
Washington, DC 20009

Mexican Tourism Office, New York
405 Park Ave., Suite 1402
New York, NY 10022

Mexican Tourism Office, Texas
5075 Westheimer, Suite 975W
Houston, TX 77056

Mexico Art and Culture Directory
http://www.mexonline.com/culture.htm
Discover how wooden toys are made, find out about rug weaving, and learn about many other Mexican arts, crafts, and celebrations.

MayaQuest
http://www.mecc.com/mayaquest.html
At this amazing web site, kids from around the world use computers to keep in contact with explorers searching for ruins of the ancient Mayan civilization.

The Art of Mexican Native Children
http://www.DocuWeb.ca/Mexico/1-engl/kids.html
Take a look at some beautiful artwork from kids who live in Mexico.

Mexico Map
http://www.lib.utexas.edu/Libs/PCL/Map_collection/americas/Mexico_rel97.jpg
Check out this online map of Mexico, provided by the University of Texas at Austin.

Glossary

ancient very old

civilization the way of life of a people

commemorate honor, celebrate

declaration statement, announcement

defeated gained victory over

empire a group of territories under a single ruler or government

enchilada a rolled, filled tortilla covered with sauce and baked

independence freedom

marvelous amazing, causing astonishment and wonder

moistened made wet

observe commemorate

pulp the soft, inner part of certain fruits and vegetables

resplendent splendid, shining brillliantly

shawl a type of clothing that you wear over your shoulders

tortilla a flat, round-shaped bread made of cornmeal or wheat flour

traditional handed down from generation to generation

Index

Look what doesn't come from Mexico!

The word "chili" comes to us from the Aztec Indians. But the delicious meal known as **chili con carne** was not invented in Mexico. It originated in the United States.

Meet the Author

Miles Harvey has written several books for young people. He lives in Chicago. This book is dedicated to Chris Kasamis and Sonia da Silva.